Starting off with

Time

Written by Peter Patilla

Illustrations by Liz Pichon

OXFORD

UNIVERSITY PRESS

OXFORD
UNIVERSITY PRESS

Great Clarendon Street, Oxford OX2 6DP

Oxford University Press is a department of the University of Oxford.
It furthers the University's objective of excellence in research, scholarship,
and education by publishing worldwide in

Oxford New York

Athens Auckland Bangkok Bogotá Buenos Aires Calcutta
Cape Town Chennai Dar es Salaam Delhi Florence Hong Kong Istanbul
Karachi Kuala Lumpur Madrid Melbourne Mexico City Mumbai
Nairobi Paris São Paulo Singapore Taipei Tokyo Toronto Warsaw

with associated companies in Berlin Ibadan

Oxford is a registered trade mark of Oxford University Press
in the UK and in certain other countries

British Library Cataloguing in Publication Data available

H/b ISBN 0–19–910663–0
P/b ISBN 0–19–910664–9

1 3 5 7 9 10 8 6 4 2

Designed and Typeset by Perry Tate Design
Printed in Hong Kong

My name is

....

Notes for parents and teachers

This book develops early concepts of *time* for adults and children to enjoy and share together. It has been carefully written to introduce the key words and ideas related to *time* which children will meet in their first couple of years in school.

Throughout the book, you will see **Word Banks** which contain the new mathematical words introduced for each concept. All the words from the word banks are gathered together at the back of the book. You can use the word banks with your child in several ways:

● See which of the words are recognized through games such as *I spy: I spy the word 'clock' – can you find it? I spy a word beginning with 'h' – where is it?*
● Choose a word and ask your child to find it in the book.
● Let your child choose a word from the word bank at the back of the book, and say something about it.

Look for other opportunities in everyday life to use the ideas and vocabulary introduced in this book. Include time words such as: quick, slow, early, late, before and after. Ask questions such as: What did we do this morning? What did we do yesterday? Ensure that children realize that maths is easy, and most importantly, fun.

A day

Each day ends at midnight.
A new day starts just after midnight.

Midnight is the time between one day and the next.
Midday is the middle of the day. It is also called noon.

Some people work during the night.
Who could they be?

Word Bank

day

night

midnight

midday

noon

Do you know of any animals that come out at night?

A week

Each week has seven days.

Here are the names for each day of the week.
The diary shows what Jo did each day in one week.

Monday

school visit

Tuesday

birthday party

Wednesday

swimming club

Thursday

visited Grandma

Friday

tidied my bedroom

Saturday

went shopping

Sunday

went to the park

We call Saturday and
Sunday **the weekend**.

Today

Wednesday

What day was it yesterday?

Today

Sunday

What day will it be tomorrow?

Which are weekend days?
Which are weekday days?
What day is it today?

Word Bank

day

weekend

diary

today

week

tomorrow

yesterday

weekday

Monday	Tuesday	Wednesday	Thursday	Friday	Saturday	Sunday

A year

A year is divided into months, weeks and days.

A year has: 12 months
52 weeks
365 days

Every fourth year has one day more. This is called a leap year. Leap years have 366 days.

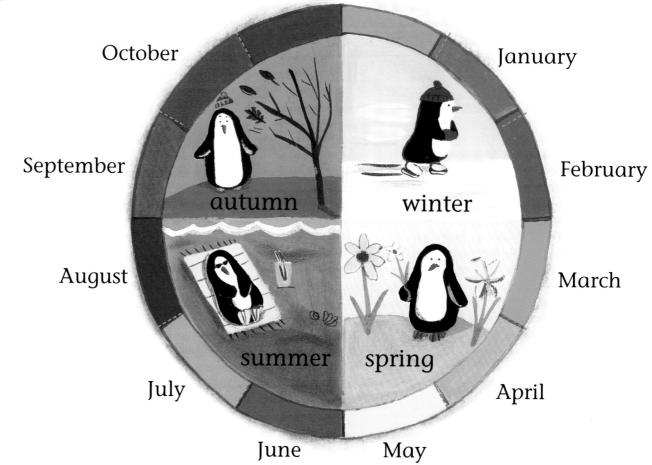

November   December

October   January

September   February

autumn   winter

August   March

summer   spring

July   April

June   May

A year has seasons. The seasons are linked to the weather.

Which seasons do you think these belong to?

In which month is your birthday?
How old are you?
How old will you be next year?

Word Bank

year   season

leap year   month   day

Getting older

As time passes things get older.

Seeds grow into plants. It can take a few months or many years.

Eggs hatch into birds. It usually takes a few weeks.

Babies eventually become adults. It takes about 18 years.

Which of these are new?

How old will each person be next year?

Word Bank

young

old

new

older

Which is the baby and which is the adult?

11

Hours, minutes and seconds

A day is divided into hours, minutes and seconds.

midnight

12 hours 12 hours

midday

One complete day is 24 hours.

It takes one hour for the big hand to move right round a clock.
One hour is 60 minutes.

A minute is divided into seconds.
There are 60 seconds in one minute.
A second is a very short time.

a minute

Which of these would you time in:

- hours? - minutes? - seconds?

sleeping

drawing a picture

Word Bank
· · · · · · · · · · · · ·
- hour
- minute
- second
- midday
- midnight

writing your name

brushing your teeth

drinking a cup of milk

watching TV

13

Clocks and watches

Clocks and watches tell us the time.

Some clocks and watches have hands. The big hand tells the minutes. The small hand tells the hours.

minute hand

hour hand

second hand

Some clocks and watches have a special hand that tells the seconds. This moves round quite quickly.

Some clocks and watches do not have hands. They have only numbers. These are called digital clocks and watches.

What is special about these clocks and watches?

What does this do in the morning?

Which noise might you hear from this clock?

Word Bank

- clock
- watch
- digital
- hour hand
- minute hand
- second hand
- pendulum

Why is a nurse's watch upside down?

What is a pendulum?

What makes a digital watch work?

Digital time

Digital clocks and watches use numbers to tell the time.

11:00 = *(clock face showing 11:00)*

11:30 = *(clock face showing 11:30)*

11:15 = *(clock face showing 11:15)*

11:45 = *(clock face showing 11:45)*

The numbers before the dots tell you the hour.
The numbers after the dots tell you the minutes past the hour.

11:53

Both clocks show 53 minutes past 11.
We say this time as eleven fifty-three.

Here are some morning times.
Which is the earliest time?
Which is the latest time?

How many minutes did it take to paint the picture?

Word Bank

digital   minute   hour   earliest   latest   past

On the hour

When the minute hand is on 12 it is something o'clock. The hour hand says which o'clock.

All these times are o'clock times.

O'clock times on digital clocks and watches end in 00.

9 o'clock

12 o'clock

Is she late for school?

Is he going to bed early?

At what time is she eating?

At what time is he playing?

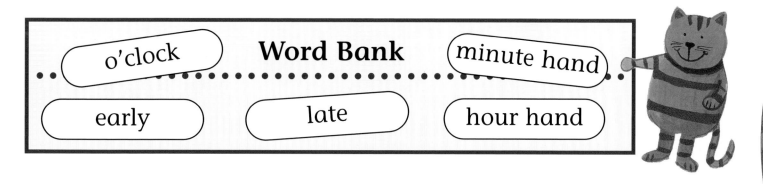

Word Bank

o'clock

minute hand

early

late

hour hand

Morning, afternoon, evening

Each day has parts called morning, afternoon and evening.

Evening is from about tea time until we go to bed.

midnight

Night time is when we are asleep in bed.

evening

early morning

afternoon

morning

Afternoon is from midday until about tea time.

midday

Morning is from when we wake up until midday.

Here is what Zig and Zog did one day.

Who went shopping in the morning?
Who had a picnic lunch?
Who wore red pyjamas in the evening?
What do you like doing in the evening?

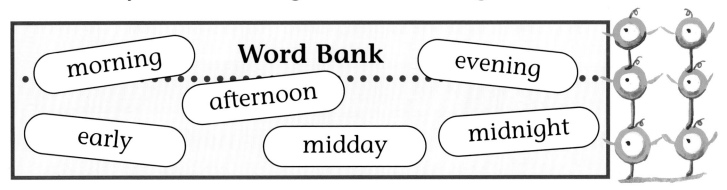

Word Bank

morning
afternoon
early
midday
evening
midnight

Half past

When the minute hand is on 6, the time says half past. The hour hand is half way between two different o'clock times.

All these times are half past times.

Half past times on digital clocks and watches end in 30.

half past nine
or nine thirty

half past twelve
or twelve thirty

At what time is each thing happening?

23

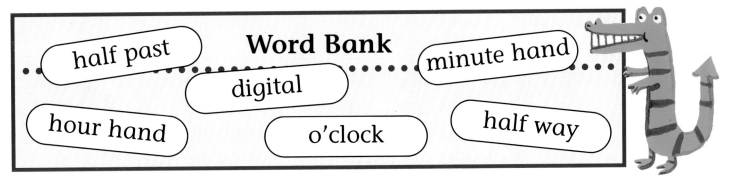

Word Bank

half past

digital

minute hand

hour hand

o'clock

half way

Minutes past

There are 5 minutes between each number on a clock face.

5:50 is nearly 6 o'clock, so the hour hand is near the 6.

Can you find pairs of clocks that show the same time?

Did you know?

The ancient Romans used the moon to help plan their calendar.

The ancient Egyptians used the sun to help plan their calendar.

Hundreds of years ago water clocks were used. Water dripped from one bowl into another. The level of water showed the time.

Candles were used as early clocks. Marks down the side showed how long the candle had been burning.

Sand timers have been used for hundreds of years to time how long things take.

Sundials were another way to tell the time. They only work in the daytime and when the sun shines.

Telling the time accurately only became necessary when trains were invented. Clocks were put on important buildings so that everyone could tell the time.

Word Bank

 night

 midnight

day

 noon

afternoon

 morning

 midday

evening

today

 morning

Play Football Today

tomorrow

28

Word Bank

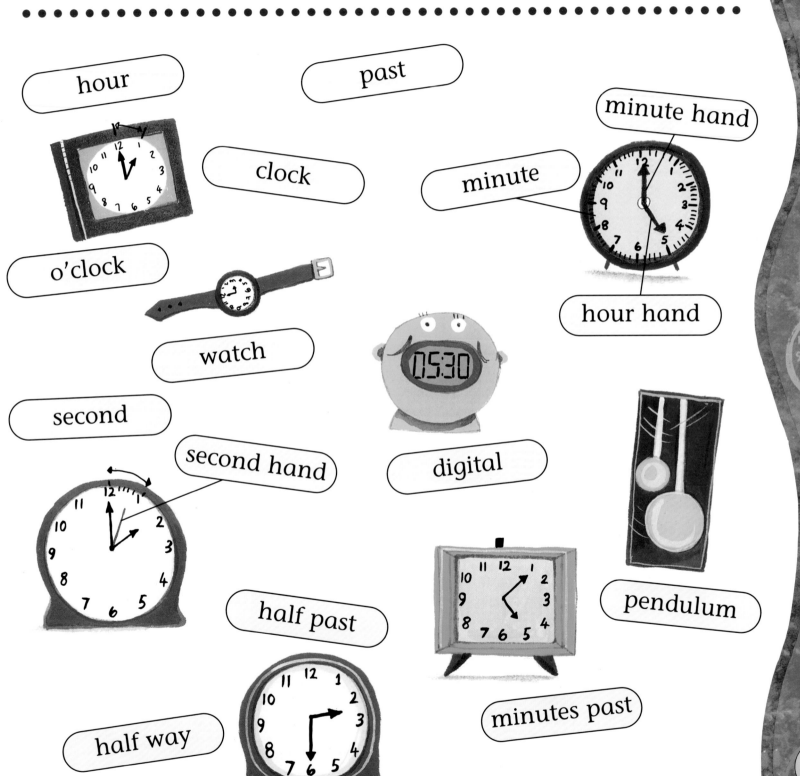

hour

past

minute hand

clock

minute

o'clock

hour hand

watch

second

second hand

digital

half past

pendulum

half way

minutes past

Word Bank

late

early

nearly

latest

earliest

old

older

new

young

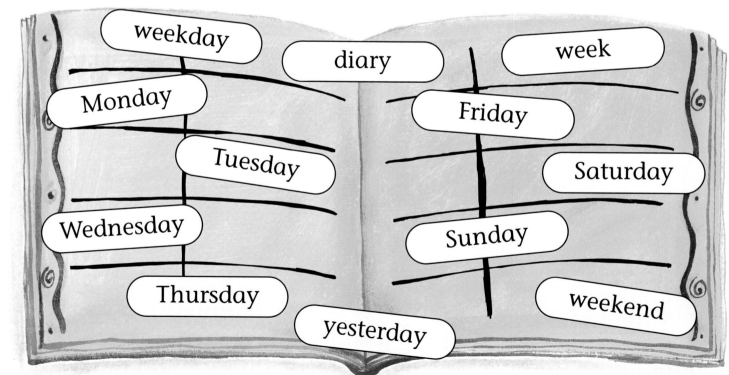

weekday

diary

week

Monday

Friday

Tuesday

Saturday

Wednesday

Sunday

Thursday

weekend

yesterday

Word Bank

month

year

season

January

February

March

April

May

June

July

August

September

October

November

December

leap year

Time Puzzle

Match each picture to a time.